The European Union

Political, Social, and Economic Cooperation

THE
EUROPEAN UNION

POLITICAL, SOCIAL, AND ECONOMIC COOPERATION

The European Union

Political, Social, and Economic Cooperation

CYPRUS

by
Kim Etingoff

Mason Crest Publishers
Philadelphia

Mason Crest Publishers Inc.
370 Reed Road, Broomall, Pennsylvania 19008
(866) MCP-BOOK (toll free)
www.masoncrest.com

First printing
1 2 3 4 5 6 7 8 9 10

Library of Congress Cataloging-in-Publication Data

Etingoff, Kim.
   Cyprus/by Kim Etingoff.
      p. cm.—(European Union: political, social, and economic cooperation)
   Includes index.
      ISBN 1-4222-0041-8
      ISBN 1-4222-0038-8 (series)

1. Cyprus. 2. Cyprus—History. 3. Cyprus—Description and travel. 4. Cyprus—Politics and government. I. Title. II. European Union (Series) (Philadelphia, Pa.)
   DS54.A3E85 2006
   956.93—dc22
                                   2005014372

Produced by Harding House Publishing Service, Inc.
www.hardinghousepages.com
Interior design by Benjamin Stewart.
Cover design by MK Bassett-Harvey.
Printed in the Hashemite Kingdom of Jordan.

Contents

THE
EUROPEAN
UNION

CYPRUS
European Union Member since 2004

Rizokarpaso

Yialousa

Akanthou

Kyrenia

Morphou

Turkish Occupied Cyprus

Lefka

Nicosia

Polis

Dhekelia

Pelendria

Larnaca

Pano Platres

Pano Lefka

Ktima

Khirokitia

Paphos

Episkopi

Limassol

Akroti

INTRODUCTION

Sixty years ago, Europe lay scarred from the battles of the Second World War. During the next several years, a plan began to take shape that would unite the countries of the European continent so that future wars would be inconceivable. On May 9, 1950, French Foreign Minister Robert Schuman issued a declaration calling on France, Germany, and other European countries to pool together their coal and steel production as "the first concrete foundation of a European federation." "Europe Day" is celebrated each year on May 9 to commemorate the beginning of the European Union (EU).

The EU consists of twenty-five countries, spanning the continent from Ireland in the west to the border of Russia in the east. Eight of the ten most recently admitted EU member states are former communist regimes that were behind the Iron Curtain for most of the latter half of the twentieth century.

Any European country with a democratic government, a functioning market economy, respect for fundamental rights, and a government capable of implementing EU laws and policies may apply for membership. Bulgaria and Romania are set to join the EU in 2007. Croatia and Turkey have also embarked on the road to EU membership.

While the EU began as an idea to ensure peace in Europe through interconnected economies, it has evolved into so much more today:

- Citizens can travel freely throughout most of the EU without carrying a passport and without stopping for border checks.

- EU citizens can live, work, study, and retire in another EU country if they wish.

- The euro, the single currency accepted throughout twelve of the EU countries (with more to come), is one of the EU's most tangible achievements, facilitating commerce and making possible a single financial market that benefits both individuals and businesses.

- The EU ensures cooperation in the fight against cross-border crime and terrorism.

- The EU is spearheading world efforts to preserve the environment.

- As the world's largest trading bloc, the EU uses its influence to promote fair rules for world trade, ensuring that globalization also benefits the poorest countries.

- The EU is already the world's largest donor of humanitarian aid and development assistance, providing 55 percent of global official development assistance to developing countries in 2004.

The EU is neither a nation intended to replace existing nations, nor an international organization. The EU is unique—its member countries have established common institutions to which they delegate some of their sovereignty so that decisions on matters of joint interest can be made democratically at the European level.

Europe is a continent with many different traditions and languages, but with shared values such as democracy, freedom, and social justice, cherished values well known to North Americans. Indeed, the EU motto is "United in Diversity."

Enjoy your reading. Take advantage of this chance to learn more about Europe and the EU!

Ambassador John Bruton,
Head of Delegation of the European Commission, Washington, D.C.

Cyrus's Troodos Mountains

CHAPTER 1

THE LANDSCAPE

Located in the crossroads between Africa, Europe, and Asia, Cyprus is a unique island country with a distinct culture, history, and geography. The tiny island in the Mediterranean Sea is roughly the size of the state of Connecticut, or about 3,571 square miles (9,250 square kilometers). It is 140 miles (225 kilometers) long at its longest point, and at its widest is about 60 miles (97 kilometers) across. Despite its small size, it is the third largest island in the Mediterranean, followed by Sicily and Sardinia, both parts of Italy. Its closest neighbors are Turkey, which is 40 miles (64 kilometers) away to the north, and Syria, 60 miles (97 kilometers) to the east.

Unfortunately, in recent years, Cyprus has gone through political turmoil. In 1974, it officially was divided into the Greek Cypriot area in the south and west, and the Turkish Cypriot area in the north and the east. A boundary, called the Green Line, separates the two regions and passes through the capital, Nicosia.

CLIMATE

Cyprus has a traditional Mediterranean climate, with moderate winters and very hot summers. The average yearly temperature is 68°F (20°C). Winter, which lasts from December to February, has an average temperature of 50°F (10°C). In the summer, temperatures commonly reach 97°F

Cyprus has a sunny climate.

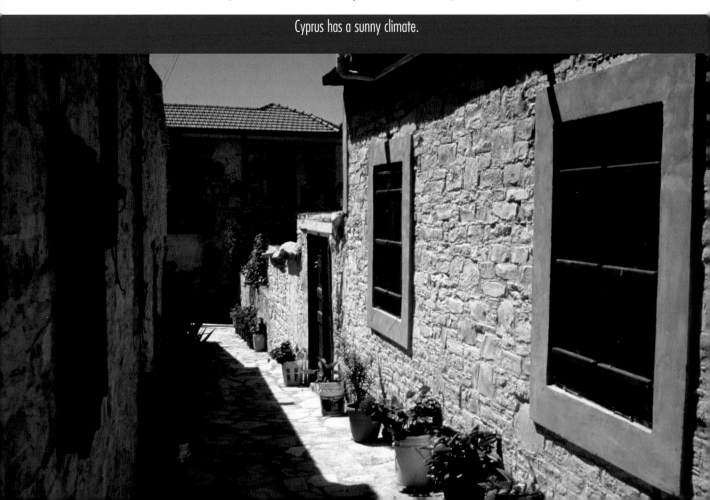

Cyprus's coastal regions are mild and breezy.

(36°C). It is usually dry throughout most of the year, with the rainy season occurring during the winter months. This short period of rain allows Cyprus to enjoy three hundred days of sunshine! Unfortunately, the lack of rain can result in a **drought**, and the people of Cyprus often have to conserve water.

The coasts of Cyprus are much milder than the inland areas. In the interior of the island, October evenings are often cool. The arrival of November brings much cooler temperatures and changes in the colors of the leaves.

The forests of Troodos

The Mountainous Regions and the Plains

Mountains make up a large portion of Cyprus. The country has two main mountain ranges: the Troodos Massif in the central and western part of the island and the Kreynian Range in the north.

The Troodos Mountains are on average 656 feet (200 meters) tall and are located in the western part of the island. They have much more vegetation than the coastal areas of the country. The Troodos are often mined for the large amounts of valuable minerals they contain, especially copper. The Kreynian Mountains are located on the northern coast of Cyprus. These mountains are made mainly from limestone. The highest mountain in this range is Mount Selvili, which is 3,357 feet (1,023 meters) high.

The Mesaoria Plain separates the Troodos and Kreynian mountain ranges. This area is slightly hilly and extremely fertile and contains most of the country's farmland and vineyards.

Coasts and Forests

Besides mountains and plains, Cyprus also has thousands of miles of coasts and forests. The coasts of Cyprus vary greatly in their appearance. Some are smooth, sandy beaches. Other coastal areas are rocky cliffs that rise out of the sea. Still other areas contain wide bays that open into the Mediterranean.

Forests are also an important feature of Cyprus. The majority of the pine forests are located on the Akamas Peninsula in the west of the island. These woods are currently part of a state forest, but it is hoped that they will soon be established as a national park.

Many acres of Cyprus's forests have been destroyed by **deforestation** due to agriculture and mining. The grazing of goats also helped destroy wooded areas. However, the people and government of Cyprus are working to protect their

> ## Quick Facts: The Geography of Cyprus
>
> **Location:** Middle East, island in the Mediterranean Sea, south of Turkey
> **Area:** about .06 the times of the state of Connecticut
> *total:* 3,571 square miles (9,250 sq. km.)
> *land:* 3,568 square miles (9,240 sq. km.)
> *water:* 3.9 square miles (10 sq. km.)
> **Borders:** none
> **Climate:** temperate; Mediterranean with hot, dry summers and cool winters
> **Terrain:** central plain with mountains to the north and south; scattered plains along southern coast
> **Elevation extremes:**
> *lowest point:* Mediterranean Sea—0 feet (0 meters)
> *highest point:* Mount Olympus—6,401 feet (1,951 meters)
> **Natural hazards:** moderate earthquake activity, droughts
>
> Source: www.cia.org, 2005.

A friendly pelican on the streets of Paphos

forests. Grazing is prohibited in certain areas, and hunting has been banned in the Paphos forest in the southwest and the woods surrounding the Troodos Mountains. Some large mines have closed, and Cyprus is committed to reclaiming this land.

FLORA AND FAUNA

Cyprus's natural environment is due largely to the fact that it is an island. Animals and plants that live in the country are often found only in Cyprus because of its isolated nature. Its location between the continents of Europe, Asia, and Africa also contribute to the large number of plants and animals that can be found in Cyprus.

Approximately 1,750 different species of plants live on the island. Of these, 168 of them are **endemic**. The plant life includes several varieties of wild flowers, irises, rock roses, crown anemones, junipers, and citrus trees.

The island is also home to a large number of birds, including the imperial eagle, Eleanora's falcon, and the griffon vulture. In all, over 350 species of birds have been spotted, due in part to the fact that Cyprus provides a good spot for migrating birds to rest.

Other types of animals also live on the island. The largest animal left in the wild is the moufflon, a type of wild sheep that can only be found in Cyprus. Foxes, hedgehogs, and fruit-eating bats also make Cyprus their home.

The Mediterranean Sea is full of animal life.

In addition to Cyprus's land animals, a wide variety of marine life live in the seas surrounding the island, including seals, dolphins, and several species of sea turtles. Several species of marine life have become endangered, however. Species such as the ghost crab, the green turtle, and the logger-head turtle are all quickly disappearing from the island because of human activities.

Reconstructions of Bronze Age homes

2 CYPRUS'S HISTORY AND GOVERNMENT

CHAPTER

Cyprus has witnessed a turbulent history for such a small island. Over the last 10,000 years, it has been occupied by numerous empires and tribes, ranging from early **hunter-gatherers**, to the ancient Egyptians, to the colonial British Empire. In more recent years, the country has become divided both politically and ethnically. Two separate countries—the Republic of Cyprus in the south and west, and the Turkish Federal Republic of Cyprus in the north and

Ancient Roman ruins near Limassol

ANCIENT CYPRUS

The history of human life on Cyprus began thousands of years ago. The first people to live arrived there around 8000 BCE. However, these hunter-gatherers appear to have been temporary inhabitants, and it was not until 7000 BCE that people began to call Cyprus their permanent home. One southern settlement, Khirokitia, was home to over 2,000 people. These people lived in two-story houses made of stone. The settlement did not last long and disappeared after a few centuries. Other small tribes and settlements quickly took the place of these people.

EUROPEAN UNION—CYPRUS

THE COPPER AND BRONZE AGES

Between the years 4000 BCE to 2500 BCE, Cyprus experienced the **Copper Age**. Many ad-vancements were made by the inhabitants of the island, including those belonging to the Ermi culture. Sculpture flourished, as well as metal-work and pottery. A new architectural style consisting of circular buildings was also introduced into several settle-ments during this period. The ruins of these ancient settle-ments can still be seen.

The **Bronze Age** immediately followed the Cop-per Age, beginning around 2500 BCE and ending in 1050 BCE. Trade with countries such as Egypt, Syria, and Crete distinguished this peri-od from those before it. Further advancements were made in the arts, especially in jewelry and bronze sculpture. The people of Cyprus also adopted a **syllabary** system of writing. This writing system has yet to be translated into mod-ern-day languages.

Over the next thousand years or so, Cyprus was conquered by the Hitittes, Assyrians, Egyptians, and the empire-builder Alexander the Great. During this period, the first Phoenicians, people from the coasts of modern-day Lebanon, and Greeks from the Peloponnese Peninsula began to settle in Cyprus. The influence these peoples had on the island can be seen in the culture and popu-lation of modern Cyprus.

DATING SYSTEMS AND THEIR MEANING

You might be accustomed to seeing dates expressed with the abbrevia-tions BC or AD, as in the year 1000 BC or the year AD 1900. For centuries, this dating system has been the most common in the Western world. However, since BC and AD are based on Christianity (BC stands for Before Christ and AD stands for *anno Domini*, Latin for "in the year of our Lord"), many people now prefer to use abbreviations that people from all reli-gions can be comfortable using. The abbreviations BCE (meaning Before Common Era) and CE (meaning Common Era) mark time in the same way (for example, 1000 BC is the same year as 1000 BCE, and AD 1900 is the same year as 1900 CE), but BCE and CE do not have the same religious overtones as BC and AD.

PEACE AND CHAOS UNDER THE ROMANS AND BYZANTINES

In 58 BCE, after Egypt was conquered, Cyprus came under the rule of the Roman Empire. The Romans brought a period of peace to the island, and Cyprus experienced increased prosperity. Ports, roads, and architecture, including theaters and **aqueducts**, were built throughout the area.

Also during this period, the island was visited by the Apostles Paul and Barnabas and was converted to Christianity.

When the Roman Empire split in 395 CE, Cyprus became part of the eastern division, the Byzantine Empire. Soon after, several earthquakes in the fourth century caused the ruin of many cities. Despite these natural disasters, Cyprus again enjoyed an era of relative serenity under Byzantine rule.

The peace of the Cypriots was quickly forgotten with the Arab raids on the island beginning in the 600s. Sometime between 647 CE and 649 CE, the Arabs attacked Constantia, then the capital of Cyprus. In the following three centuries, dozens of cities were destroyed, and thousands of people were killed or sold into slavery.

In 965, the Byzantine Empire was able to regain the island. Another period of peace prevailed. Trade again flourished, and several impor-

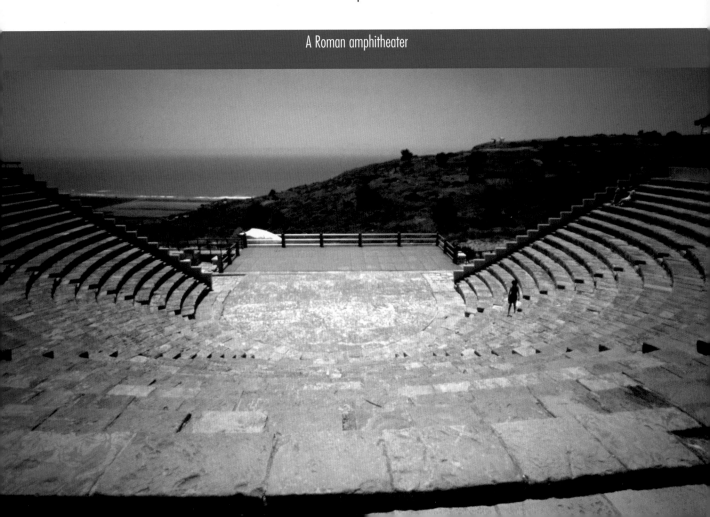

A Roman amphitheater

The Arabs destroyed Roman cities and temples.

tant churches were built, such as that of St. Barnabas in Salamis and St. Lazarus in Larnaca.

Following the island's pattern of alternating periods of prosperity and disorder, this peace was soon shattered. In 1171, Isaac Comnenos, a Byzantine governor, seized power over the empire, along with Cyprus. He ruled the country with violence and force and was considered a *tyrant* by his subjects, who suffered under his government.

ENGLISH RULE

In 1191, the English king Richard the Lionheart defeated Comnenos and took control of Cyprus, which was a strategic base used during the

Crusades. After overthrowing Comnenos, Richard demanded that the Cypriots pay him a large amount of money. Unhappy with this burden, the people rebelled. Although this uprising was easily crushed, Richard sold the island, which had become too much of a problem, to the Knights Templar.

The Knights Templar was an organization formed to protect Christians during the Crusades. Their brief rule was marked by excessive force, especially when putting down rebellions of the Cypriots. The Knights Templar eventually abandoned Cyprus, and the island was sold to the Frankish Guy de Lusignan in 1192. Lusignan, who had previously been king of Jerusalem, lost the island to the Venetians in 1489.

In 1571, the island yet again changed hands, this time to the Ottoman Turks. Cyprus passed through more than three centuries of Turkish rule until the island was **ceded** to Britain in 1878.

When World War II broke out, Cypriots for the most part sided with the Allies. Although the island was never directly involved in the war, it served as an air base and several thousand of its citizens served under the British and Greek armies.

THE DIVISION

During the period of British rule, Greek-Cypriots began expressing their desire for *enosis*, or union with Greece, especially during the 1930s. The movement, led by the EOKA (National

A medieval castle in Paphos

Modern Cyprus

Organization of Cypriot Fighters) reached a peak in the 1950s under its director, Archbishop Makarios. The Turkish-Cypriots who also lived on the island were alarmed at the **escalation** of the movement and had no desire for enosis, but on August 16, 1960, Cyprus gained its independence from Britain, and the Greek-Cypriots elected Archbishop Makarios as the new country's president.

In 1974, however, Makarios was overthrown by a military **junta** and was forced into exile. Turkey soon sent troops to Cyprus, hoping to take advantage of the chaos created by the situation. Turkish troops soon had control of the northeastern portion of the island.

In November 1983, the Turkish third of the island officially declared itself the Turkish Republic of Northern Cyprus. The only country that has formally recognized it is Turkey. Meanwhile, the Republic of Cyprus, which controls the southwestern two-thirds of the island, is the internationally recognized government of the island. Almost all foreign governments, as well as the United Nations, recognize the **sovereignty** of the Republic of Cyprus over the whole island of Cyprus.

The United Kingdom also still has territory on Cyprus. Under the independence agreement made in 1960, the United Kingdom retained the title to two small areas on the southern coast of the island, known collectively as UK sovereign base areas. They are used to host military bases.

MODERN CYPRUS

The division of the island and the violence that accompanied it took a toll on both new countries. The Republic of Cyprus was able to successfully improve its economy, but the Turkish Republic was not quite as successful. Both relied—and still rely—on the tourist industry. The Republic of Cyprus also instituted a modern educational system, as well as a health-care system, both of which helped to improve the **standard of living** of Greek-Cypriots.

Today, the Republic of Cyprus is a true republic. The president of the country is elected every five years. A parliament, made up of fifty-six representatives, also elected every five years, constitutes the legislative branch of the government. All adult Cypriots have the right to vote.

Cyprus has come a long way from an island of hunter-gatherers. The effects of the recent violence and disruption resulting from the division of the country are still felt, but the Republic of Cyprus is proving that recovery can be achieved. It is now a country with a stable government and a relatively strong economy.

Artichoke fields near Larnaka

3 THE ECONOMY

The Republic of Cyprus has made a miraculous and remarkably fast recovery from the turmoil that rocked the country during the 1970s. Since its political division, it has surpassed the economic growth of the Turkish Republic of Cyprus to the north, and has established itself in the world mar-

A WESTERN ECONOMY

Cyprus's successful economy is proven. Its **gross domestic product (GDP)** is $9.7 billion, the sixteenth highest GDP **per capita** in the world. In addition, it currently has a relatively low rate of unemployment and little **inflation**.

This success can be attributed to the policies chosen after the Turkish-Cypriots broke away from the south. A **market economy** was created in the republic, providing a good base for a flourishing economy. An educated labor force and a spirit of **entrepreneurship** have added to the growth of the economy.

AGRICULTURE

Agriculture has been, and still is, a vital part of the economy of Cyprus. Citrus fruits, potatoes, and grapes are among its agricultural exports. In addition, the fertile land also supports carrots, tomatoes, almonds, bananas, olives, artichokes, and **legumes**.

Wine production is a particularly significant industry. Grapes grow well, especially in the southwest of the island. Approximately four-fifths of all grapes grown in Cyprus are used for the making of wine. Two-thirds of that wine is exported.

MANUFACTURING AND TRADE

The Republic of Cyprus has become increasingly dependent on manufacturing and industry as it moves into modern times. Currently, it exports products such as pharmaceuticals, cement, clothing, processed foods, and paper. Its manufacturing industry is now only second to its **service industry** based on tourism.

Agriculture plays a vital role in Cyprus's economy.

However, Cyprus still depends on other countries for the goods it cannot produce. Its imports include petroleum and other fuels that are not available locally, machinery, and transportation equipment. It relies heavily on European countries for much of its needs, especially those countries belonging to the European Union (EU).

RESOURCES AND ENERGY SUPPLIES

Cyprus has very limited energy resources because of its geography and its position as an island. No fuels can be found naturally, which makes it necessary to import fuels such as petroleum in order to sustain the country. Petroleum alone accounts for approximately 95 percent of Cyprus's energy consumption. The country also lacks rivers that could be used to generate hydroelectric power in the absence of petroleum.

Fortunately, Cyprus does have two valuable sources of energy: firewood and sunlight. Wood is a traditional source of energy, but as forests are

A dam on one of Cyprus's few rivers

The Cyprus government is dedicated to reclaiming the land from the former asbestos mine in the Troodos Mountains.

being depleted, the people of Cyprus have become less dependent on wood and have turned to solar energy instead. Many houses are equipped with solar panels that capture the abundant sunlight and convert it into electricity.

The island is also very rich in minerals, especially copper that can be found under the Troodos Mountains. Other minerals that have been mined on Cyprus include asbestos, chromite, gypsum, and iron pyrite. The mineral industry has declined in recent decades because of the depletion of the ores. It received a particularly heavy blow when the asbestos mine was closed in 1988.

Cyprus's many Roman ruins draw tourists from around the world.

TRANSPORTATION

As a relatively modern country, much of Cyprus has up-to-date transportation systems. Most of the main roads on the island are paved and offer easy access to cities and large towns. However, the numerous smaller roads that branch off the main arteries are often unpaved.

Cyprus also has two international airports: Larnaka and Paphos. Seaports are also available, such as the ones at Larnaka, Limassol, and Paphos. These ports and airports are the only legal ports of entry into the country.

LINGERING PROBLEMS

Although Cyprus has a booming economy, it is not as stable as those of many other countries. Its economy is highly dependent on the island's tourist industry, which is subject to fluctuations. Many tourists are discouraged from traveling to Cyprus because of the tensions between the Republic of Cyprus and its neighbor to the north, the Turkish Republic of Cyprus.

Cyprus's well-being is also dependent on the economies of Western European nations, with whom it trades extensively. If the economies of these nations take a downturn, Cyprus's economy does as well.

A young boy rides his bike on the streets of Limmasol.

CYPRUS'S PEOPLE AND CULTURE

The two distinct groups of people living on Cyprus are separated not only by political boundaries but by ethnicity, language, and religion as well. Approximately 77 percent of Cyprus's population is Greek and 18 percent are Turkish, leaving only 5 percent who can claim a different ethnic background. The Greeks descend from the Peloponnesian immigrants who arrived on the island around 1200 BCE and

Quick Facts: The People of Cyprus

Population: 780,133 (July 2005 est.)
Ethnic groups: Greek 77%. Turkish 18%, other 5% (2001 estimates)
Age structure:
  0-14 years: 20.9%
  15-64 years: 67.7%
  65 years and above: 11.4%
Population growth rate: 0.54%
Birth rate: 12.57 births/1,000 pop.
Death rate: 7.64 deaths/1,000 pop
Migration rate: 0.43 migrants/1,000
Infant mortality rate: 7.18 deaths/1,000 live births
Life expectancy at birth:
  Total population: 77.65 years
  Male: 75.29 years
  Female: 80.13 years
Total fertility rate: 1.83 children born/woman
Religions: Greek Orthodox 78%, Muslim 18%, Maronite, Armenian Apostolic, and other 4%
Languages: Greek, Turkish, English
Literacy rate: 97.6% (2003 est.)

Note: All figures are 2005 estimates unless otherwise noted.
Source: www.cia.gov, 2005.

Turks in the northeast. The people of Cyprus speak either Greek or Turkish, depending on their ethnicity. Many can also speak English.

Religion

The vast majority of Greek-Cypriots belong to the Greek Orthodox church, while more Muslims live in the island's northeast. However, freedom of religion is guaranteed for all Cypriots, and small numbers of people are Maronite, Armenian Orthodox, and Roman Catholic.

Cyprus was once an important center of early Christianity. In 45 CE, it was one of the first places visited by the Apostles St. Paul and St. Barnabas. The island was later able to claim independence from the Byzantine Church on the basis that St.

assimilated themselves with the local native population. The Turks can be traced back to soldiers from the Ottoman Empire and to later Turkish immigrants.

Because of their differences, these two groups are divided between their respective countries, with the Greeks living in the southwest and the

Barnabas founded the Church of Cyprus. It has retained this title until today, and the Archbishop of Cyprus is still allowed certain privileges. Today's Cypriots are proud of this distinction.

HEALTH CARE

The people of Cyprus enjoy a well-established and effective system of medical care, which is overseen by the Ministry of Health. Health services are free for the poor and are available at reduced rates for the middle class. Six general hospitals have been built in the island's cities. Rural health centers provide care for those unable to get to these hospitals. Improvements in medical care over the past few decades have caused a dramatic

The moasque in Larnaka marking the birthplace of Mohammed's mother draws Muslim pilgrims. Each cloth tied to the tree symbolizes a prayer.

increase in life expectancy, as well as a decrease in the infant mortality rate.

The government also offers several other services. Among them are child day care, retirement homes, care for the disabled, and shelters for refugees.

EDUCATION

The Ministry of Education and Culture oversees Cyprus's very advanced educational system. Education is **compulsory** between the ages of five and fifteen. Six years each of primary and secondary schooling is provided for all children. Almost 100 percent of all children attend school, contributing to Cyprus's almost 98 percent rate of **literacy**. The University of Cyprus is available for further education, along with technical and **vocational** schools.

FOOD

Food found in Cyprus is a unique blend of Turkish and Greek. Some of the most popular dishes are *mezedes*, which consist of up to twenty or thirty small dishes of different foods, including, but not limited to, feta cheese, tomatoes, olives, smoked ham, fish, stuffed grape leaves, and hummus (a dip made from ground chick peas). Traditionally, Cypriots enjoy savoring their meal, so a *meze* can last for a long time.

Coffee shops, located in virtually every village, are an essential part of life on Cyprus. Cafés, or *kafenios*, are considered the centers of

A Cypriot woman demonstrates traditional lace making.

Cypriots celebrating Palm Sunday, the week before Easter

village life. Greek coffee is served in these kafenios, but customers can also order tea and fresh juice made from local fruits.

FESTIVALS

Many of the festivals celebrated on Cyprus are related to religion. The most important holiday of the year is the Greek Orthodox Easter, which holds more significance on Cyprus than Christmas. Many people begin celebrating by attending church on the Saturday before Easter. A bonfire is lit outside the church after the mass, and fireworks are set off.

Individual towns throughout the island often celebrate specific seasons. Springtime signifies carnivals and parades of floats made from flowers. At the fall harvest time, many small wine festivals are held, celebrating one of the island's favorite industries. Limassol hosts both the largest spring carnival and the most extravagant wine festival.

ARTS AND CRAFTS

Traditional crafts are still a large presence on the island. Intricate lace making is very prevalent among the women, while men participate in silver crafts. These arts are especially popular with tourists. However, as Cyprus moves into modern times, these crafts are in danger of dying out. Most of the younger generation of Cypriots is uninterested in continuing their elders' work and prefer finding jobs in other fields.

Limassol's harbor

5 THE CITIES

With the decline in agriculture in recent years, more and more Cypriots have moved from the country to urban areas. This became especially apparent in the years after World War II. However, many people who now work in cities can commute to work and are able to settle close-by in smaller towns or in more rural

The cities of Cyprus captivate both native Cypriots and tourists. Most are the descendants of earlier cities and still contain remnants of their earlier glories. Today, they are modern and vibrant places to live and work.

NICOSIA

Although Nicosia is the capital of the Republic of Cyprus, part of the district in which it is located, also called Nicosia, belongs to the northeastern Turkish Republic of Cyprus. A portion of the city itself is contained in the buffer zone set up between the two countries by the United Nations.

As the capital, Nicosia is an important trade and manufacturing center. Textile, leather, and plastic industries are all situated in the city. Copper mines can also be found in close proximity to the city.

Nicosia has a rich history that is reflected in its buildings and ruins. The thirteenth-century Church of St. Sophia, which is now a **mosque**, holds the remains of the kings and queens of the Lusignan dynasty who once ruled the island. The remains of old Venetian structures and buildings are also present.

LIMASSOL

Limassol is the second-largest city in Cyprus. It is also a major seaport and resort that attracts many of the tourists who vacation on the island. Although it caters to these tourists, with restaurants, shopping, and a busy nightlife all avail-

An open-air market in Nicosia

The legendary birthplace of Aphrodite, the goddess of love

able, it also contains a rich history. The city was the sight of Richard the Lionheart's famous marriage to Berengaria and became his center of command on the island.

The city is also archaeologically important. Excavations that have taken place have revealed that Limassol is the site of two ancient cities, Kourioin and Amathous, which held much power. One ancient ruin, the Kourion Theatre, is still used today for concerts and plays.

PAPHOS

Paphos is currently the fourth-largest city in Cyprus. It was originally the capital and kept that title for almost eight hundred years. It was an important trading city in the time of the Romans, but has been subject to frequent earthquakes throughout its history.

Paphos (often spelled Pafos) is sometimes considered to be the birthplace of Aphrodite, the Greek goddess of love. It is said that she arose out of the sea near the present-day city, making it a popular site of *pilgrimage* with ancient Greeks. Today, the ruins of the Temple of Aphrodite, built in the twelfth century BCE, can still be seen.

LARNAKA

Another of Cyprus's major seaports and tourist destinations is the city of Larnaka. This city is home to one of the island's two international airports. Besides being a popular vacation spot, Larnaka has a history of being an important religious spot.

Larnaka's busy beachfront

The Church of St. Lazarus, dedicated to the early saint of the same name, still stands, as does Stavrovouni Monastery, one of the oldest monasteries on the island.

The EU flag

6 THE FORMATION OF THE EUROPEAN UNION

The EU is an economic and political confederation of twenty-five European nations. Member countries abide by common foreign and security policies and cooperate on judicial and domestic affairs. The confederation, however, does not replace existing states or governments. Each of the twenty-five member states is *autonomous*, but they have all agreed to establish some common institutions and to hand over some of their own decision-making powers to these international bodies. As a result, decisions on matters that interest all member states can be made democratically, accommodating everyone's concerns and interests.

Today, the EU is the most powerful regional organization in the world. It has evolved from a primarily economic organization to an increasingly political one. Besides promoting economic cooperation, the EU requires that its members uphold fundamental values of peace and **solidarity**, human dignity, freedom, and equality. Based on the principles of democracy and the rule of law, the EU respects the culture and organizations of member states.

HISTORY

The seeds of the EU were planted more than fifty years ago in a Europe reduced to smoking piles of rubble by two world wars. European nations suffered great financial difficulties in the postwar period. They were struggling to get back on their feet and realized that another war would cause further hardship. Knowing that internal conflict was hurting all of Europe, a drive began toward European cooperation.

France took the first historic step. On May 9, 1950 (now celebrated as Europe Day), Robert Schuman, the French foreign minister, proposed the coal and steel industries of France and West Germany be coordinated under a single supranational authority. The proposal, known as the Treaty of Paris, attracted four other countries—Belgium, Luxembourg, the Netherlands, and Italy—and resulted in the 1951 formation of the European Coal and Steel Community (ECSC). These six countries became the founding members of the EU.

In 1957, European cooperation took its next big leap. Under the Treaty of Rome, the European Economic Community (EEC) and the European Atomic Energy Community (EURATOM) were formed. Informally known as the Common Market, the EEC promoted joining the national economies into a single European economy. The 1965 Treaty of Brussels (more commonly referred to as the Merger Treaty) united these various treaty organizations under a single umbrella, the European Community (EC).

In 1992, the Maastricht Treaty (also known as the Treaty of the European Union) was signed in Maastricht, the Netherlands, signaling the birth of the EU as it stands today. **Ratified** the following year, the Maastricht Treaty provided for a central banking system, a common currency (the euro) to replace the national currencies, a legal definition of the EU, and a framework for expanding the

The EU's united economy has allowed it to become a worldwide financial power.

EU's political role, particularly in the area of foreign and security policy.

By 1993, the member countries completed their move toward a single market and agreed to participate in a larger common market, the European Economic Area, established in 1994.

The EU, headquartered in Brussels, Belgium, reached its current member strength in spurts. In

© BCE ECB EZB EKT EKP 2002

200

© BCE ECB EZB EKT EKP 2002

100

© BCE ECB EZB EKT EKP 2002

50

© BCE ECB EZB EKT EKP 2002

20

The euro, the EU's currency

1973, Denmark, Ireland, and the United Kingdom joined the six founding members of the EC. They were followed by Greece in 1981, and Portugal and Spain in 1986. The 1990s saw the unification of the two Germanys, and as a result, East Germany entered the EU fold. Austria, Finland, and Sweden joined the EU in 1995, bringing the total number of member states to fifteen. In 2004, the EU nearly doubled its size when ten countries—Cyprus, the Czech Republic, Estonia, Hungary, Latvia, Lithuania, Malta, Poland, Slovakia, and Slovenia—became members.

THE EU FRAMEWORK

The EU's structure has often been compared to a "roof of a temple with three columns." As established by the Maastricht Treaty, this three-pillar framework encompasses all the policy areas—or pillars—of European cooperation. The three pillars of the EU are the European Community, the Common Foreign and Security Policy (CFSP), and Police and Judicial Co-operation in Criminal Matters.

QUICK FACTS: THE EUROPEAN UNION

Number of Member Countries: 25
Official Languages: 20—Czech, Danish, Dutch, English, Estonian, Finnish, French, German, Greek, Hungarian, Italian, Latvian, Lithuanian, Maltese, Polish, Portuguese, Slovak, Slovenian, Spanish, and Swedish; additional language for treaty purposes: Irish Gaelic.
Motto: *In Varietate Concordia* (United in Diversity)
European Council's President: Each member state takes a turn to lead the council's activities for 6 months.
European Commission's President: José Manuel Barroso (Portugal)
European Parliament's President: Josep Borrell (Spain)
Total Area: 1,502,966 square miles (3,892,685 sq. km.)
Population: 454,900,000
Population Density: 302.7 people/square mile (116.8 people/sq. km.)
GDP: €9.61.1012
Per Capita GDP: €21,125
Formation:
- Declared: February 7, 1992, with signing of the Maastricht Treaty
- Recognized: November 1, 1993, with the ratification of the Maastricht Treaty

Community Currency: Euro. Currently 12 of the 25 member states have adopted the euro as their currency.
Anthem: "Ode to Joy"
Flag: Blue background with 12 gold stars arranged in a circle
Official Day: Europe Day, May 9.

Source: europa.eu.int

PILLAR ONE

The European Community pillar deals with economic, social, and environmental policies. It is a body consisting of the European Parliament, European Commission, European Court of Justice, Council of the European Union, and the European Courts of Auditors.

PILLAR TWO

The idea that the EU should speak with one voice in world affairs is as old as the European integration process itself. Toward this end, the Common Foreign and Security Policy (CFSP) was formed in 1993.

PILLAR THREE

The cooperation of EU member states in judicial and criminal matters ensures that its citizens enjoy the freedom to travel, work, and live securely and safely anywhere within the EU. The third pillar—Police and Judicial Co-operation in Criminal Matters—helps to protect EU citizens from international crime and to ensure equal access to justice and fundamental rights across the EU.

The flags of the EU's nations:

top row, left to right
Belgium, the Czech Republic, Denmark, Germany, Estonia, Greece

second row, left to right
Spain, France, Ireland, Italy, Cyprus, Latvia

third row, left to right
Lithuania, Luxembourg, Hungary, Malta, the Netherlands, Austria

bottom row, left to right
Poland, Portugal, Slovenia, Slovakia, Finland, Sweden, United Kingdom

ECONOMIC STATUS

As of May 2004, the EU had the largest economy in the world, followed closely by the United States. But even though the EU continues to enjoy a trade surplus, it faces the twin problems of high unemployment rates and **stagnancy**.

The 2004 addition of ten new member states is expected to boost economic growth. EU membership is likely to stimulate the economies of these relatively poor countries. In turn, their prosperity growth will be beneficial to the EU.

THE EURO

The EU's official currency is the euro, which came into circulation on January 1, 2002. The shift to the euro has been the largest monetary changeover in the world. Twelve countries—Belgium, Germany, Greece, Spain, France, Ireland, Italy, Luxembourg, the Netherlands, Finland, Portugal, and Austria—have adopted it as their currency.

SINGLE MARKET

Within the EU, laws of member states are harmonized and domestic policies are coordinated to create a larger, more-efficient single market.

The chief features of the EU's internal policy on the single market are:

- free trade of goods and services

- a common EU competition law that controls anticompetitive activities of companies and member states

- removal of internal border control and harmonization of external controls between member states

- freedom for citizens to live and work anywhere in the EU as long as they are not dependent on the state

- free movement of **capital** between member states

- harmonization of government regulations, corporation law, and trademark registration

- a single currency

- coordination of environmental policy

- a common agricultural policy and a common fisheries policy

- a common system of indirect taxation, the value-added tax (VAT), and common customs duties and **excise**

- funding for research

- funding for aid to disadvantaged regions

The EU's external policy on the single market specifies:

- a common external **tariff** and a common position in international trade negotiations

- funding of programs in other Eastern European countries and developing countries

COOPERATION AREAS

EU member states cooperate in other areas as well. Member states can vote in European Parliament elections. Intelligence sharing and cooperation in criminal matters are carried out through EUROPOL and the Schengen Information System.

The EU is working to develop common foreign and security policies. Many member states are resisting such a move, however, saying these are sensitive areas best left to individual member states. Arguing in favor of a common approach to security and foreign policy are countries like France and Germany, who insist that a safer and more secure Europe can only become a reality under the EU umbrella.

One of the EU's great achievements has been to create a boundary-free area within which people, goods, services, and money can move around freely; this ease of movement is sometimes called "the four freedoms." As the EU grows in size, so do the challenges facing it—and yet its fifty-year history has amply demonstrated the power of cooperation.

Europe is proud of its "bright idea," a union with economic and political power.

The EU believes that it can use its power to act as a "lighthouse" for the rest of the world.

KEY EU INSTITUTIONS

Five key institutions play a specific role in the EU.

THE EUROPEAN PARLIAMENT

The European Parliament (EP) is the democratic voice of the people of Europe. Directly elected every five years, the Members of the European Parliament (MEPs) sit not in national **blocs** but in political groups representing the seven main political parties of the member states. Each group reflects the political ideology of the national parties to which its members belong. Some MEPs are not attached to any political group.

COUNCIL OF THE EUROPEAN UNION

The Council of the European Union (formerly known as the Council of Ministers) is the main leg-

islative and decision-making body in the EU. It brings together the nationally elected representatives of the member-state governments. One minister from each of the EU's member states attends council meetings. It is the forum in which government representatives can assert their interests and reach compromises. Increasingly, the Council of the European Union and the EP are acting together as colegislators in decision-making processes.

EUROPEAN COMMISSION

The European Commission does much of the day-to-day work of the EU. Politically independent, the commission represents the interests of the EU as a whole, rather than those of individual member states. It drafts proposals for new European laws, which it presents to the EP and the Council of the European Union. The European Commission makes sure EU decisions are implemented properly and supervises the way EU funds are spent. It also sees that everyone abides by the European treaties and European law.

The EU member-state governments choose the European Commission president, who is then approved by the EP. Member states, in consultation with the incoming president, nominate the other European Commission members, who must also be approved by the EP. The commission is appointed for a five-year term, but can be dismissed by the EP. Many members of its staff work in Brussels, Belgium.

COURT OF JUSTICE

Headquartered in Luxembourg, the Court of Justice of the European Communities consists of one independent judge from each EU country. This court ensures that the common rules decided in the EU are understood and followed uniformly by all the members. The Court of Justice settles disputes over how EU treaties and legislation are interpreted. If national courts are in doubt about how to apply EU rules, they must ask the Court of Justice. Individuals can also bring proceedings against EU institutions before the court.

COURT OF AUDITORS

EU funds must be used legally, economically, and for their intended purpose. The Court of Auditors, an independent EU institution located in Luxembourg, is responsible for overseeing how EU money is spent. In effect, these auditors help European taxpayers get better value for the money that has been channeled into the EU.

OTHER IMPORTANT BODIES

1. European Economic and Social Committee: expresses the opinions of organized civil society on economic and social issues

2. Committee of the Regions: expresses the opinions of regional and local authorities

3. European Central Bank: responsible for monetary policy and managing the euro

4. European Ombudsman: deals with citizens' complaints about mismanagement by any EU institution or body

5. European Investment Bank: helps achieve EU objectives by financing investment projects

Together with a number of agencies and other bodies completing the system, the EU's institutions have made it the most powerful organization in the world.

EU Member States

In order to become a member of the EU, a country must have a stable democracy that guarantees the rule of law, human rights, and protection of minorities. It must also have a functioning market economy as well as a civil service capable of applying and managing EU laws.

The EU provides substantial financial assistance and advice to help candidate countries prepare themselves for membership. As of October 2004, the EU has twenty-five member states. Bulgaria and Romania are likely to join in 2007, which would bring the EU's total population to nearly 500 million.

In December 2004, the EU decided to open negotiations with Turkey on its proposed membership. Turkey's possible entry into the EU has been fraught with controversy. Much of this controversy has centered on Turkey's human rights record and the divided island of Cyprus. If allowed to join the EU, Turkey would be its most-populous member state.

The 2004 expansion was the EU's most ambitious enlargement to date. Never before has the EU embraced so many new countries, grown so much in terms of area and population, or encompassed so many different histories and cultures. As the EU moves forward into the twenty-first century, it will undoubtedly continue to grow in both political and economic strength.

Cyprus's beaches draw tourists from the rest of the EU.

7 CYPRUS IN THE EUROPEAN UNION

Cyprus is one of the newest members of the EU. It became a member state in May 2004, along with nine other countries. Of these ten countries, Cyprus is considered to have the most advanced economy. Since it is such a new member, however, the country has not had much time or opportunity to participate in the EU's policies and governmental

RELATIONSHIP WITH THE EU

Cyprus has received financial aid from the EU during the latter part of the twentieth century. Since 1973, the EU has provided funding for structural and economic improvements, including upgrades in electricity, water purification, and sewage systems. Loans were also made available to Cyprus from the 1970s until the 1990s.

The EU has also been one of Cyprus's main trading partners. Over 50 percent of its trade is conducted with members of the EU. Since Cyprus has historically been so interwoven with the EU, it was almost inevitable that Cyprus would eventually apply for membership.

THE CYPRUS PROBLEM

Cyprus officially applied for membership in the EU in 1990. However, there were many ***reserva-***

A street player in Paphos earns his living from tourists who flock to Cyprus from other nations in the EU.

An open-air market displays traditional sweets.

tions among member states over admitting Cyprus. The main uncertainty shared by many countries was the divided nature of Cyprus: the Turkish Federal Republic in the northeast and the Greek Republic in the southwest.

Those arguing for the annexation of both parts of the island believed that membership would help the island as a whole. The countries would be allowed to work out their differences in a peaceful manner under the watch of the EU. The EU would also be in a better position to help the poor economy of northeastern Cyprus if it belonged to the organization. More money, including loans and aid, would be made available for improvements in the country's floundering economy.

Nicosia's modern streets are divided by the Green Line, separating the Republic of Cyprus from Turkish-occupied territory.

The EU allowed negotiations for Cyprus's membership on the condition that the Turkish and Greek countries continue their discussions of a political peace treaty. It was also hoped that current efforts by the United Nations would help bring this about. The EU then declared that Cyprus would only be allowed to join if it reached this peace agreement.

The EU eventually cancelled this condition. It decided to allow the **accession** of the Republic of Cyprus in the Greek portion of the island. This was based both on the fact that the Turkish Republic was not internationally recognized as a country and because of the difficulties in uniting the two opposing countries.

PRE-ACCESSION AND INITIATION

Formal negotiations concerning Cyprus's membership began in 1995. Since then, Cyprus has been striving to change its policies in order to fit in with those of the EU. The money needed for this job has been partially provided for by the EU itself. Fifty-seven million euros, to be used over five years (from 2000 to 2004), was given to Cyprus for this purpose.

On April 16, 2003, Cyprus signed the Accession Treaty in Athens. The next step was official recognition as a member state, which occurred on May 1, 2004.

A glimpse into Cyprus's peace, a peace that is disturbed by Turkish occupation.

Cypriots
and Their Future in the EU

Emphasis is often placed on the governments of countries, but the people of those countries must be considered too. In this case, Greek-Cypriots are very excited to have become citizens of the EU. They recognize the political, economic, and social benefits that the EU offers, including increased trade and job opportunities.

Turkish-Cypriots also desire to become part of the EU. In a poll conducted in 2003, 77 percent of all Turkish-Cypriots indicated they favored joining the EU. In addition, 36 percent of them said they favored politically joining with the rest of the island.

Both ethnic groups are able to see the value of cooperation and unity. Each country fears what further division will do to their countries, especially economically. While this is apparent to the people, this is not always the case with their governments or the governments of other countries. Turkey has long pushed for continued division. The political leader of the Turkish Republic also stands in the way of unity and peace.

However, Turkey is also seeking admission to the EU. To do so, its government will have to work toward a peaceful resolution to Cyprus's division. Meanwhile, more and more people in Cyprus are beginning to realize the benefits of unity. Clearly, if all Cypriots are willing to work toward a unified country, both in and out of the EU, they will be able to achieve it in the near future.

A Calendar of Cypriot Festivals

January: January 1, **New Year's Day**, is celebrated much like the American Christmas. Ayios Visilios, the Cypriot version of Santa Claus, gives children gifts on this day. Epiphany, an important Greek Orthodox holiday, is observed on January 6 and marks the end of the holiday season.

March: The date of **Green Monday**, which is celebrated on the first Monday of **Lent**, varies from year to year and can also be celebrated in February. Picnics of bread, olives, and vegetables are often prepared.

April: Greek Orthodox Easter (which can be celebrated in March) is the most important celebration of the year. People generally attend church, and then gather around large bonfires. On Easter Sunday, many people eat roast lamb.

June: Seaside towns observe **Kataklysmos**, the festival of the flood, on June 7.

July: July 20 is **Peace and Freedom Day**, marking the anniversary of the Turkish invasion in 1974.

October: Independence Day is celebrated on October 1. On October 28, Greek-Cypriots observe **Greek National Day**, showing the deep connections to Greece that still exist.

December: The Christmas season begins on December 6, with the **Feast of St. Nicholas**. Although **Christmas** is celebrated on December 25, it is not as important as Easter. It is mainly a religious holiday, but it is also celebrated with Christmas carnivals and a turkey dinner.

Loukoumades
(Cinnamon and Honey Fritters)

Makes 12 servings

Ingredients
About 1/2 ounce fresh yeast, or 1/5 ounce dried yeast
1 cup warm water
1/2 teaspoon sugar
8 ounces plain flour
1/4 teaspoon salt
1 cup corn oil, for frying
cinnamon
honey

Directions
Dissolve the fresh yeast in half a teacup of the warm water. Add the sugar to it, to activate, and let it stand in a warm place for about 15 minutes, until it starts to froth. Sift the flour and salt into a bowl and empty the dissolved yeast or the dried yeast into it, mixing continuously. Start adding the rest of the warm water, beating all the time. The mixture should be thick but elastic. When almost all the water has been added, beat it for a few minutes until it starts to bubble. Cover the bowl with a thick towel and leave in a warm place for about 2 hours, until it rises and almost doubles in size. Have a cup of cold water ready, which you can wet a spoon and your fingers in. Heat the oil until very hot but not smoking. Wet the teaspoon so that the dough will not stick on it. Using a spoon, drop a small amount of dough into the oil (take care not to burn yourself). Within seconds it puffs up and rises to the surface. Repeat this process, wetting the spoon each time, making a batch of 6 to 7 loukoumades at a time. Turn them over so they become golden all around—it only takes 1 minute. Take them out with a slotted spoon and drain on a paper towel. Serve loukoumades with honey and cinnamon. Eat them immediately.

Horiatiki
(Greek Salad)

Ingredients
4 tomatoes, sliced in segments
1 onion, sliced
1/2 sliced cucumber
lemon juice
chopped parsley and/or coriander
sliced feta cheese (a white, salty cheese made with goat's milk)
olives
salt, pepper, and oregano for seasoning
olive oil

Directions
Mix the vegetables, lemon juice, parsley, cheese, and olives together. Pour olive oil over them and sprinkle on salt, pepper, and oregano.

Tzaziki

Ingredients
18 ounces of Greek yogurt (or natural full-fat, dairy yogurt)
3 garlic cloves
1/2 cup of olive oil
1/2 sliced cucumber

Directions
Put the yogurt in a bowl. Put the garlic through a garlic press, and using the edge of a knife, spread the garlic coming out of the press on the yogurt. Take the cucumber and peel the skin. Slice it thinly. Mix the ingredients with a mixer (or a fork) and slowly add the oil. The oil will be absorbed, and when it is, the tzaziki is ready. Serve with a few olives spread on the top, and eat with a spoon.

Nut-Stuffed Semolina Pastries, Cyprus Style

Makes 30 servings

Ingredients
1/4 pound sweet butter
1 1/4 cup fine semolina
orange flower water
1/4 teaspoon salt
3 tablespoons warm water (more if needed)
1 cup chopped unsalted pistachios
4 1/2 tablespoons granulated sugar
1 tablespoon ground cinnamon
confectioners' sugar

Directions
In a small, heavy saucepan, bring the butter to a bubble over medium heat and stir in the fine semolina. Transfer to a small bowl, cover, and let stand overnight at room temperature. The next day, uncover and add 2 teaspoons orange flower water and the salt. Gradually add the warm water, working with your fingers to make a firm dough. Knead for 5 minutes, then cover and let rest 1 hour. Meanwhile, combine the pistachios, sugar, and ground cinnamon in a small bowl. Break off pieces of dough slightly larger in size than a walnut, and form into a ball. Press the center with your thumb to make a large well and fill with 1 teaspoon of the nut mixture, then cover over with dough and shape into an oval. Set on a cookie sheet and continue until all pastries are shaped. Bake at 350°F for 30 to 35 minutes, or until the yellow color has become lighter. Cool for 10 minutes, then dip quickly into orange flower water and roll in confectioners' sugar. Cool before storing.
Note: You may substitute blanched almonds for the pistachios and peanut oil for the butter.

PROJECT AND REPORT IDEAS

Maps

- Draw a map of Cyprus, including the major cities. Be sure to indicate the line between the Republic of Cyprus and the Turkish Federal Republic.
- Create an export-import map of Cyprus and the rest of Europe, using arrows to indicate the products that are exported and imported.

Reports

- Write a brief report on the early missionary trip of Paul and Barnabus to Cyprus.
- Write a report on the Roman Empire's role in Cyprus.

Journals

- Imagine you are a young person growing up in one of the Copper Age round houses. Describe what your life is like.
- Imagine that you are a young person living in a Roman colony on Cyprus at the time of the fourth-century earthquake. Describe the events that took place and the effect they had on your daily life.

Projects

- Learn the Greek and Turkish expressions for simple words such as hello, good day, please, and thank you. Try them on your friends.
- Make a travel poster describing one of Cyprus's tourist attractions.

Group Activities

- Debate: One side should take the role of the Greek Cypriots and the other the Turkish Cypriots. Each side should defend its point of view in reference to the unification of Cyprus.
- Host a typical Cyprus meal, with many small dishes (mezedes).

CHRONOLOGY

8000 BCE	Hunter-gatherers inhabit the island.
7000 BCE	Permanent settlers arrive on the island.
4000–2500 BCE	Copper Age.
2500–1050 BCE	Bronze Age, advanced city-states emerge.
1500 BCE	Hittite rule begins.
1450 BCE	Egyptians take control of island.
850 BCE	Assyrian rule begins, and Cyprus experiences a golden age.
525 BCE	Persian rule, also called the Cypro-Classical period, begins.
58 BCE–395 CE	Roman Empire rules the island.
395 CE	Cyprus becomes part of the Byzantine Empire.
c.600 CE	Arab attacks on the island begin.
965	Byzantines regain island and peace is reestablished.
1191	Richard the Lionheart of England occupies Cyprus.
1192	Cyprus sold to Guy de Lusignan.
1489	Control of island passes to Venetians.
1571	Ottoman Turks begin to rule.
1878	Cyprus comes under British domination.
1960	Independence from Britain is achieved.
1974	Turkey invades Cyprus.
1975	Northern portion of the island is declared the Turkish Federal Republic of Cyprus.
1990	Cyprus formally applies for EU membership.
1995	EU membership negotiations formally begin.
2004	Cyprus becomes a member of the EU.

Further Reading/Internet Resources

Hellander, Paul. *Lonely Planet: Cyprus.* Oakland, Calif.: Lonely Planet Publications, 2003.
Lerner Publishing Group. Cyprus *in Pictures.* Minneapolis, Minn.: Author, 1992.
Spilling, Michael. *Cyprus*, 2nd ed. Tarrytown, N.Y.: Marshall Cavendish, 2000.
Streissguth, Thomas. *Cyprus: Divided Island.* Minneapolis, Minn.: Lerner Publishing Group, 1998.

Travel Information
www.traveltocyprus.com.cy
www.worldtravelguide.net/data/cy[p/cyp.asp

History and Geography
cybersleuth-kids.com/sleuth/Geography/Europe/Cyprus
www.infoplease.com/ipa/A0107447.html
www.workmail.com/wfb2001/cyprus/cyprus_history_index.html

Culture and Festivals
www.cyprus.com/cyprus-culture-traditions-and-customs.php
www.cyprusisland.com/01_Information/culture.htm

Economic and Political Information
earthtrends.wri.org/text/economics-business/country-profile-47.html
www.cia.gov/cia/publications/factbook/geos/cy.html

EU Information
europa.eu.int

FOR MORE INFORMATION

Embassy of the Republic of Cyprus
2211 R Street, NW
Washington, DC 20008
Tel.: 202-462-5772
Fax: 202-483-6710
e-mail: info@us.cyprusembassy.org

Cyprus Tourism Organisation
Leoforos Lemesou 19
PO Box 24535
1390 Nicosia, Cyprus
Tel.: 269 (22) 1100
e-mail: cytour@cto.org.cy

Embassy of the United States-Nicosia
Metochiou & Ploutarchou Streets
2407, Engomi
Nicosia, Cyprus
Tel.: 357 (22)393-939

European Union
Delegation of the European Commission to the United States
2300 M Street, NW
Washington, DC 20037
Tel.: 202-862-9500
Fax: 202-429-1766

GLOSSARY

accession: The formal acceptance by a state of an international treaty or convention.

aqueducts: Pipes or channels constructed for moving water to a lower level, often across long distances.

assimilated: Integrated someone into a larger group so that differences are minimized or eliminated.

autonomous: Able to act independently.

blocs: United groups of countries.

Bronze Age: A historical period approximately between 3500 and 1500 BCE that was characterized by the use of bronze tools.

capital: Wealth in the form of money or property.

ceded: Surrendered or gave up land, rights, or power to another country or group.

compulsory: Required by law.

Copper Age: A transitional period of history when metal tools were used alongside stone ones, and appearing in only part of the world.

Crusades: Military expeditions made by European Christians in the eleventh and thirteenth centuries to retake areas captured by Muslim forces.

deforestation: The removal of trees from an area of land.

drought: A long period of extremely dry weather and not enough rain for the successful growing of crops.

endemic: Used to describe a species that is confined to a particular geographical region.

entrepreneurship: Willingness to take on the risks and responsibilities of starting a business.

escalation: The act of increasing in intensity or number.

excise: A type of tax on domestic goods.

gross domestic product (GDP): The total value of all goods and services produced within a country in a year.

hunter-gatherers: Members of a society in which people live by hunting and gathering only, with no crops or livestock raised for food.

inflation: An economic period during which the supply of money exceeds the supply of available goods.

junta: A group of military officers who have taken control of a country following its overthrow.

legumes: A plant that has pods as fruits and roots that are used as food.

literacy: The ability to read and write at a functional level.

market economy: An economy in which prices and wages are determined by the market and the law of supply and demand.

mosque: Muslim place of worship.

per capita: By or for each person.

pilgrimage: A journey to a holy place for religious reasons.

ratified: Officially approved.

reservations: Doubts that prevent complete agreement to or approval of something.

service industry: A business that provides a service rather than goods.

solidarity: Harmony of interests and responsibilities among individuals in a group.

sovereignty: Supreme authority.

stagnancy: A state of inactivity.

standard of living: Someone's level of material comfort.

syllabary: A set of written characters in which each character represents a single syllable.

tariff: A tax levied by a government on goods, usually imports.

tyrant: A person who exercises authority unjustly and oppressively.

vocational: Relating to education designed to provide the necessary skills for a particular job.

INDEX

Picture Credits

Benjamin Stewart, Harding House photographer, traveled to Cyprus to take the photos found in this book, with the exception of the following:

Used with the permission of the European Communities: pp. 54–55, 57, 60, 63, 64

Photos.com: pp. 58, 66

Biographies

Author

Kim Etingoff currently lives in Vestal, New York, where she has lived for most of her life. She contributes to a small local newspaper, where she holds the position of editor-in-chief. A recent trip to Europe helped to foster her interest in other countries, cultures, and peoples.

Series Consultant

Ambassador John Bruton served as Irish Prime Minister from 1994 until 1997. As prime minister, he helped turn Ireland's economy into one of the fastest-growing in the world. He was also involved in the Northern Ireland Peace Process, which led to the 1998 Good Friday Agreement. During his tenure as Ireland's prime minister, he also presided over the European Union presidency in 1996 and helped finalize the Stability and Growth Pact, which governs management of the euro. Before being named the European Commission Head of Delegation in the United States, he was a member of the convention that drafted the European Constitution, signed October 29, 2004.

The European Commission Delegation to the United States represents the interests of the European Union as a whole, much as ambassadors represent their countries' interests to the U.S. government. Matters coming under European Commission authority are negotiated between the commission and the U.S. administration.